WORLD OF SOFT

If everything is Soft in this World, Peace and Prosperity should prevail. But there Hard things too !! A Software thinks and directs a Hardware. Soon it is going to happen that the Hardware will intake, digest and self-utilise the Software to drive hard the world and the human beings !!!

This Book is For

- ❖ Every House hold to know what is a Software and Hardware
- ❖ Students and Career Makers in Computer Systems and Software.
- ❖ Parents to guide their children in Their Computer oriented Career
- ❖ Teachers & Professors to indoctrinate practical guidelines for their students.
- ❖ Schools, Colleges, Universities and Other Government / Private Institutions to design and update their course contents and Syllabus.
- ❖ Institutional and Public Libraries to extend a book of practical know how in Computer Systems and Software.
- ❖ Government and Corporate Offices and other Work locations, as a reference to innovative, be productive in practical application areas for Computer Systems Design.

✳ ✳

WORLD OF SOFT

CONTENTS

SEQ	SB	LV	MATTER	PAGE
			Foreword by the Author	1
			From the Motorship	2
			From Viewer's View	2
			Software innovations of the Author	3
			Key Words	3
			JEL Classification Codes	3
01			Preface	3
02			Hardware	4
	A		Comparison to Day to Day Life	5
03			Software	7
	A		Operating System & Booting Software	7
	B		Utility Software	7
	C		Application Software	8
		1	Characteristics of an Ideal Application Software	8
		2	Characteristics of Design Methodology	9
		3	Ready made Application Software	10
		4	In-house Application Software	
04			Application Software Quality Policy of the Author	11
05			Background know-how of the Author	12
06	A		Application Software by Utility	13
	B		Application Software by Specialised Jobs	14
	C		Application Software by Organisation	16
	D		Kadayam Kasthuri Kalyani	20

WORLD OF SOFT

CONTENTS (Continued)

SEQ	SB	LV	MATTER	PAGE
07			Hard and Softwares are like Twin Towers	21
08			Published Paper – 5th Generation Computers	23
09			Corporate Infrastructure – Inferences & Support	33
	A		Upto 4th Generation – Horizontal Integration	33
	B		Actual 5th Generation Infrastructure in 1990s	34
	C		5th Generation Infrastructure Inferences	35
10			Socio-Economic Implications of Combrain	36
11			Bibliography	49
12			Feed-back through Author's Web site	50
13			About the Author	56
14			Author's other Books	57

WORLD OF SOFT

FOREWORD BY THE AUTHOR

Flower, Plants and Pot are all <u>Hardwares</u>, which can be seen, touched, felt, lifted and moved. But how to arrange the flowers and plants inside the pot, needs an education or knowledge. That knowledge or methodology can be understood and implemented, but cannot be seen as a hard object. However that procedure can be only documented, for reference and use. Hence it is called a <u>Software</u>, and it works through a <u>memory</u>.

As soon as a baby <u>fish</u> comes out of a tiny egg, under the sea, it knows how to swim ! When a <u>Calf</u> is born to a Cow, it knows how to suck the milk from the mother, how to getup and attempt to walk !! A <u>plant</u> grows into a tree and knows how to spread its roots deep into the earth to fetch the water !!! These knowledge pool are recorded and implanted into the <u>brain</u> (chemical memory) of the new born, or the <u>seeds</u> of a tree. These are softwares written and recorded by the nature. Hence the Software exists from the day of <u>evolution</u> of life in this universe, with a general rule that it needs a <u>living</u> matter to use and act upon.

But the human brain innovated methodologies to <u>eliminate</u> the need for a life to use and act upon the instruction of a software, as well as to <u>convert</u> a software into a hardware. It is a <u>Computer</u> or an automated <u>machine</u> tool or a <u>Robot</u>. In an Air craft it is an Auto-<u>Pilot</u>, in a ship it is a Self-<u>navigator</u>, in the machine shop it is a <u>numerically</u> controlled boring machine, in an air conditioner it is a <u>thermostat</u> etc... But a software <u>directing</u> a hardware <u>without</u> a living matter to <u>control</u> it from behind, <u>cannot</u> take corrective actions to situations not provided to think for the best alternative !!!

Hence, the persons <u>behind</u> the computers or machines should be very clear about the Hardware, the techniques to <u>develop</u> or <u>purchase</u> a quality/fool-proof software, and the methodology to assess the <u>performance</u> of both. Also, it may be a good guideline to know the range of Software by Utility, Specialised jobs and Organisations.

****

WORLD OF SOFT

From The Motor Ship, The Marine Technology Magazine, UK. June 2003. Page 10. News. Advisories. "Distraction of Technology"

It is the IT age and computers are supposed to solve our every need. Yet the <u>grounding</u> of a vessel in restricted waters off western <u>Scotland</u> has led to the ship's owner having all computers <u>removed</u> from the bridges of its <u>entire</u> fleet. The 4,500 Kg cargo ship ran <u>aground</u> on a clear summer's morning after its <u>automatic</u> steering <u>failed</u> to implement a planned <u>change</u> of course. The Officer-On-Watch (OOW) had been left <u>alone</u> on the bridge...The master was asleep at the time, and having been woken by the <u>impact</u> made his way to the bridge where he found the OOW holding the steering joystick with the steering switched to <u>manual</u> control. It took <u>four</u> days to re-<u>float</u> the ship and it suffered substantial bottom <u>damage</u>.... A report of the incident, published by the Marine Accident <u>Investigation</u> Branch of Transport says ".... The decision taken by the ship's owner to <u>remove</u> computers from the bridges of all their vessels, is seen as a <u>positive</u> step".

<u>From Viewer's Views @ www.dvsrs.com</u>

As soon as I <u>bought</u> my <u>Lap Top</u>, I <u>started</u> with Windows and Autocad. So I was feeling that <u>software</u> is a <u>box</u> or a <u>chip</u> inside a computer, made of <u>soft</u> materials. John Derik Christoffer, Sweden.

When a Personal Computer (<u>PC</u>) or <u>Laptop</u> is purchased, the current <u>commercial</u> practice <u>includes</u> the price with <u>licensed</u> versions of Windows, Games, Internet Browsers, Videos, Techno-commercial Design Software etc...as a package. These are <u>pre-recorded</u> on the hard <u>disc</u> and <u>delivered</u> to the customers. Many buyers <u>feel</u> that the <u>pre-recorded</u> software as a <u>pre-set</u> hardware chips. Hence, Software is <u>not</u> a "Magic box". But it is an <u>intricately</u> assembled "Logic Cox" ! (<u>Logic</u> = Orderly <u>directions</u> given to do a job. <u>Cox</u> = A <u>head</u> of a race or boat crew, with certain <u>targets</u>). But with the <u>advancement</u> in <u>electronic</u> technology, the <u>software</u> codes are <u>converted</u> into "<u>Plug and Play</u>" micro chips. The best <u>examples</u> are the software logic of a Calculator, Game, Virus Scan etc.. are available on micro <u>chips</u> and <u>inserted</u> into the <u>computer</u> or <u>Video</u> Cassette <u>Players</u>. Hence these <u>Logic Coxes</u> are becoming <u>Magic Boxes</u>. **Dr.VSRS**

WORLD OF SOFT

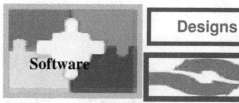

SOFTWARE INNOVATIONS OF THE AUTOR

KEY WORDS
Application, Assumption, Audit, Background, Booting, Computer, Corporate, Design, Expectation, Flexible, Hardware, Hybrid, Imagination, Inferences, Infrastructure, In-house, Integrated, Intelligent, Interface, Jobs, KKK, Know-how, Knowledge, Logic-Cox, Magic-Box, Modification, Operating-System, Organisation, Plug and Play, Precaution, Productive, Published-Paper, Quality, Rate of Return, Ready-Made, Service, Software, Specialised, Speed, Support, Tower, Understanding, Utility, Views, Viewers, Voice-Processing, Wafer-Scale.

JEL CLASSIFICATION CODES
C88, D78, L15, L86, M41, M42, M53, O32

01. PREFACE

- <u>From Holy Quran</u>
- **Contrast is understood by Even and Odd (Sura Al-Fajr 89-03).**
- **Glory of Allah who created in pairs all things that the Earth produces as well as their own (human) kind and (Other) things which they have no knowledge (Sura Ya-Sin 36-36)**
- **Praise to Allah who created Heavens and the Earth, And made the Darkness and the Light (Sura Al-Anam 06-01)**

- <u>Albert Einstein</u>
  (Nobel Laureate in Physics 1921 for his Theory of Relativity)
- **Time and Space (Dual existence) are Curved and United into one.**

In the Light of knowledge attained, the happy achievements seems to be almost a matter of course, and any intelligent student can grasp it without too much trouble. But the years of anxious searching in the Dark, with their intensive longing for their alterations of confidence and exhaustion, and final emergence into the Light, only those who have experienced it can alone understand it

WORLD OF SOFT

<u>From Thaithriya Upanishad</u>

- To identify the Truth, one should be clear about what is Falsehood.
- To perceive the value of Light, one should be able to encompass the feelings of darkness.
- To understand the effect of Eternity, one should know what is the impact of destruction..

02. <u>HARDWARE</u>

As highlighted in the preface, <u>contrast</u> is needed for a clear understanding and knowledge of any matter, because every thing in the universe is relational.

- To understand the Softness, we should talk of Hardness, because it is visible, can be felt, quantifiable and measurable.
- But a Hardware like nuts, bolts, scales, thermometer etc... has no life or any intrinsic quality or hidden value attached to it.
- They <u>only</u> perform the function for which they are designed, and as per directions from an external <u>environment</u> plus an <u>animate character</u> (with life - human or animal etc...) behind it, and who handles it.
- <u>Computer</u> or any auto-controlled machine like a <u>Refrigerator</u>, is a Hardware with a special function to perform namely to think, act, signal, repeat and whenever necessary, with a combination of Audio-Video and Electro-magnetic communication interface (Internet).

- It cannot perform these functions <u>unless</u> it is directed by an external <u>environment</u> plus an <u>animated character</u> (with life - human) behind it, and who handles it.

02A. CONPARISON TO DAY TO DAY LIFE

IN OUR KITCHEN			IN OUR COMPUTER		
Ser#	ITEMS	CALLED	ITEMS	CALLED	Ser#
01	Pans, Plates, Stove etc	Vessels	Processor Unit, Key Board, Mouse etc...	Hardware	A
02	Gas, Oil etc...	Cooking Media	Disk, Diskette,CD etc..	Electronic Media	B
03	Starting and Pre-heating, before food making	Initialisation	Starting and preparing the machine before job work	Operating System and Booting Softwares	C
04	Common additives like Salt, Spices etc...	Taste additives	Tables, Graphs etc..presentation options	Utility Softwares	D
05	Needed Recipe	Cooking and Preparation Methodology	User Needs	Application Software	E
06	Person preparing	Cook	Person starting and controlling the machine to function as desired.	Administrator Systems Analyst , Programmer, Operator	F
07	Persons Eating	Guests	Persons getting informations and using it	Users	G

01. In the <u>Kitchen</u> environment, if any body claims that buying a popular <u>brand</u> of any <u>one</u> or <u>combination</u> of items from 01 to 05 can guarantee a tasty food, can it be true ? NO, because there are 2 hidden elements called Preparation Skill, and the Taste / Liking of a given group of guests, which <u>change</u> from time to time, and from group to group.

- So also is the Computer Environment. Any single or combination of popular items A to E, <u>cannot</u> meet the needs of any given set of users, because the expectations are different, infrastructure / operating environments are different, and they change from time to time to synchronise with the altered environments.

02. In the <u>Kitchen</u> environment, if any body claims he / she is a Good Cook and can make tasty food, it cannot be taken for granted. Because, the assorted taste and expectations of the Guests cannot be quantified and conveyed by any body to the cook.

- So also is the Computer Environment. Any single or combination of personnel (Item F) <u>cannot</u> meet the needs of any given set of users. Because there are hidden elements like job knowledge, ability to translate the user requirements into Computer language etc...Also, the expectations of the users, change from time to time, and there should be an after-development support to meet these changing requirements, for continued and productive use.

In the above Home and Computer comparison diagram, items C, D and E falls in to the category of Software.

03. SOFTWARE

03A. OPERATING SYSTEM / BOOTING SOFTWARE

This is a prime need to start / prepare the computer and hand over the machine to the user. The important aspect of this Software should be to control and direct the use of,

❖ **Make the computer work for any <u>Utility</u> Software like**

- Word Processor (to write letters etc..),
- Spread sheet (to tabulate informations, present graphically etc...),
- A net-work (communicate and share informations from other computers in the neighbourhood)
- Browser (to initiate the Internet and communicate with the world).

❖ **Understand and make the computer perform the desired functions of any <u>Application</u> Softwares, one has to learn and develop in-house (home or office..).**

- Commercial applications - Accounting, Stocks, Manpower oriented jobs.
- Technical Applications - Production planning, In-process control etc..
- Special Applications - Telex, Fax, Email, Art, Drawing, Games etc...

Hence, it is beyond the scope of any user to prepare this <u>Operating System</u> software, because of the complexity of its integration with the Hardware circuit specifications, and fast changing electronic technology. It is bought along with a given computer hardware combinations, works exclusively for that machine (or similarly configured machines).

03B. UTILITY SOFTWARE

Once there is a computer and an Operating System Software, it is very handy to buy certain Utility Softwares, compatible to the given configuration, They are,

- Word Processor (to write letters etc..),
- Spread sheet (to tabulate information, present graphically etc...),
- A net-work (communicate and share informations from other computers in the neighborhood)

- Browser (to initiate the Internet and communicate with the world).
- Games.
- Other Musical, Drawing, Art etc...

But these are designed by somebody, sitting somewhere, with certain pre-set assumptions of a variety of users, in their imagination. Hence, one has to operate within the limitations or the flexibility provided by these Softwares.

If anybody claims that buying and use of these Utility Softwares can improve the productivity, efficiency and profitability of your organisation, please do not take it for granted. Because,

1. Your individual and organisational needs will be definitely different from the general assumptions behind these Utilities.
2. The information to be given in, and the expected result representations will be changing from time to time. But these Utilities cannot be modified by you.
3. Any information cannot be standardised globally due to geographical, monetary, social set-up of the work-force, and the socio-economic conditions of operation, which are not common.
4. You and your organisation should bend and fit into the requirements and limitations of the Utility. It ends in the persons serving the Utility, than the Utility serving the persons.

03C. APPLICATION SOFTWARE

The Application Softwares are those which will make the computer execute jobs needed by you and your organisation.

There is a common tendency among the users all over the world, to take advantage of the Utility Softwares explained above, to perform the applications like Accounts, Manpower, Sales jobs etc...But these are performed within lot of limitations and constraints in-built, in these utilities.

03C1. Characteristics of an ideal Application Software

- In-take one information from one point, and utilise it for many information needs, to a variety of users (Duplication of data entry should be eliminated)

- At the entry point of information, all possible errors should be highlighted and eradicated (Data entry edits and corrections).
- Adequate help should be provided to the data entry as well as user personnel to search and get the correct information, with least difficulty (on-line effects).
- Wherever possible the computer should auto-generate the common and contra data (Speedy operations).
- Automated audit of information entered should be available (Detect and Fix wrong information due to Hardware failure, possibly due to power fluctuations or virus etc...).
- Comprehensive test of the Software, prior to production and utility. (Response to different combination of conditions and the type of information)
- Support to modify the Software, as and when the information in, and out specifications are changed (Service the Software for continued use).

03C2. Characteristics of Design Methodology.

- Compatible to the operating system and network links.
- A selected programming Language OR a Software design base, which provides a platform to create a Software.
- Have the in-built professional job knowledge.
- Provide for in-house modifications, as and when required.
- At least one main plus one back-up person to know, understand and modify the Software, as and when the need arises..

03C3. Ready made Application Softwares.

Actually an Application Software is an interface-ware between the information entered (input), how they are processed (computations), and how they are presented (output).

There are many Software houses to manufacture specific Application Softwares for plug and play use. These are also Application oriented general purpose Utility Softwares.

If anybody claims that buying and use of these Softwares can improve the productivity, efficiency and profitability of your organisation, please do not take it for granted. Because,

A) Your individual and organisational needs will be definitely different from the general assumptions behind these Softwares.

B) The informations to be given in, and the expected result representations will be changing from time to time. But these Softwares cannot be modified by you.

C) Any information cannot be standardised globally due to geographical, monetary, social set-up of the work-force, and the socio-economic conditions of operation, which are not common.

D) You and your organisation should bend and fit into the requirements and limitations of these Softwares, ending up in the personnel serving the Software, than the Software serving the personnel.

This will lead any individual or organisation into loops and troubles, as well as misguide / mislead with wrong information generated by the various pre-set modules.

03C4. In-house Application Softwares.

There are 5 sets of inter-action and know-how required for in-house Software Persons (A Systems Analyst and a Programmer who design the logical instructions or Algorithms) in the Application Software.

41. Should have a clear understanding of the Inputs and the Data Entry Personnel orientations.

42. Should have a clear understanding of the Outputs and the User needs.

43. Optimum File and Data structure organisation.

44. The programming technique (Modules) to instruct the computer to covert the Inputs into desired outputs.

45. Thorough Job knowledge.

In practice the Software person attempts / understands items 41 and 42. Partially or fully conversant in 43 / 44. But lack item 45, the thorough Job Knowledge.

The Input / User personnel possess items 41, 42 and 45, but do not have any idea of item 43 / 44 the Data Organisation / Programming techniques, the computer capabilities and characteristics of an ideal Application Software as outlined in 03C1 above

These lacunae are sufficient to produce faulty and unproductive Application Software. Hence the details in 03C1 to 03C4 above are Productive Precautions to be taken before either buying or designing an Application Software.

04. APPLICATION SOFTWARE QUALITY POLICY OF THE AUTHOR

A. Computer and Software should meet the needs and requirements of the Users, than the users becoming a slave of the Hard and Software constraints.

B. Every Software should be specific user oriented, and attempt should not be made to design a General purpose Software, and fit the customers into the constraints and limitations.

C. Thorough knowledge and understanding of the inputs, outputs, processing complexities, user's hardware / software / manpower / monetary budget / infrastructure / communication and environment set-up.

D. Synchronised Input screen formats with documents.

E. Reduce and integrate the input data to a minimum and at one point.

F. Share the data already entered at different data-entry and user points.

G. In-house Software support and Training for continued and productive utility should be ensured.

H. Organise the File formats and data structures optimally for faster / Multi access, with least corruption possibilities and with field modification flexibility.

I. Choose the best and simplest programming language or Software generation utility, with modification flexibility.

J. Pre-test the Software with a minimum of 100 input data combinations with Correct and Error conditions.

K. Multi-year and Multi-company processing at any point of time.

L. Auto generate the needed entries, wherever possible and to other group companies on inter-company data entry.

M. On line search / help facilities and eliminate errors at the first entry point.

N. Organised data backup and data security facilities.

O. Integrated Digital, Audio and Video processing facilities.

P. Export and Import data to / from any General purpose Utility or through a ASCII (American Standard Code for Information Interchange) Text format.

Q. Experience gaining interface for the computer, in order to provide a valuable and intelligent on-line feed-back to the input and user personnel.

R. Knowledge based Computer utility to provide directions and guide-lines for the betterment and progress of the users.

S. Implement the Software in User location for a minimum period of 3 Months and provide a Warranty and Support for 1 Year.

T. Evaluate Economic, Financial and Social Rate of Return on the Software Investment, and provide a justification prior to the design and implementation..

U. Auto Audit by the computer to cross check and highlight its own errors if any. Process a self corrective action by the computer or suggest manual correction methods.

05. BACKGROUND AND KNOW-HOW OF THE AUTHOR

REFERENCE : Corporate Infrastructure for Fifth Generation Computers.

• Based upon a survey of Computer Hardware / Software Developments in USA and Japan

• Published by the author in Indian Management, Journal of the All India Management Association,   New Delhi, India, June 1985. Page 19 - 28.

1. The Application Softwares Designed by the Author are divided and presented   under 3 classifications, by Utility, Specialised Jobs and Organisation categories, to expose the span of Software coverage as well as to highlight the range of computer utility in the current Techno-Commercial infrastructure.

2. Programming languages used are vicious versions of ALGOL, AUTO-CODER, BASIC, C (++) COBOL, FORTRAN, PL, RPG, VISUAL SERIES ETC...

3. Software generator Utilities are wide versions of ACCESS, C++, DBASE, FOXBASE, FOXPRO, VISUAL BASIC, ORACLE etc...
4. Data Interface are vicious versions of EXCEL, LOTUS, Variety of WINDOWS, AUDIO / ARTISTIC / DRAWING / PHOTOGRAPHIC / WORD PROCESSORS etc...
5. Computers and Operating Systems are variety of versions of APPLE, COMPAQ, DATA GENERAL, IBM, ICL, NCR, Micro Soft etc..
6. Internet page generation utilities like Frontpage, HTML, Java Script etc...
7. Main frames, Mini, Personal and Desk Tops.

06A. APPLICATION SOFTWARES BY UTILITY

Applicable to Diversified Sectors

A. Integrated Resource Management.

(Financial, Material, Machinery, Manpower, and other Resources with Resource Mix and Optimisation Links)

❖ Management Methodology Modification.

1. Channel and Sources Utility.
2. Demand and Supply Mix Moderation.
3. Replacement and Design Updating Strategies.
4. Training Interfaces.

❖ Organisational Structure Tuning.
❖ Rate of Return - Economic, Financial and Social.

B. Marketing Management and Distribution Economics.

❖ Feed-back to pre / post production environments.
❖ Integrated and interfaced Socio-Economic and Marketing Data Base for

1. Customers and Organisational needs integration.
2. Diversification.

3. Leadership in Competitive environment.
4. Opportunity / Precaution Guidelines.
5. Production Planning.
6. Promotional Strategies

❖ Marketing Resource Optimisation.
❖ Reduction in Marketing Expenses.

C. Production Planning, Control & Appraisal Systems linked to

❖ Cost Reduction
❖ Experience gain and Forward Planning.
❖ Resource (Labour, Machinery, Materials) selection, utility and optimisation.

D. Qulality Oriented Systems

❖ Experience data base for Research and Development.
❖ Labour, Machinery, Materials and Supplier Ratings.
❖ Make or Buy Decisions.
❖ Value Analysis.
❖ Variety Reduction and Standardisation.
❖ Wastage Reduction.

06B. APPLICATION SOFTWARES BY SPECIALISED JOBS

A. ACADEMIC INSTITUTIONS

- In-house, Inter and Intra Bibliographic search base.
- Inter institution information exchange.
- On-line Student Progress Information base for faster performance upgrade.
- On-line parent interaction and feed back base.
- Financial modules for fee control and institution accounting

B. AGRICULTURE

- Crop Mix and Soil Fertility Maintenance.
- Crop and Service animal mix model for profitability.
- Farm output optimisation.
- Fertiliser utility and effect analysis.

C. HATCHERY AND GENETIC ENGINEERING

- Broiler / Layer experience data base for Genetic Upgrade.
- Extension of Chicken hatchery information methodology to other Animal and Plant genetic applications
- Pure-line information and Pedigree output optimisation.

D. HOSPITAL AND HEALTH MANAGEMENT.

- Health hazard location, prediction and action guidelines.
- Research and Development Data Base and Analysis based on Multi-various combinations of
    1. Diagnostic Informations
    2. Drug applications
    3. Environments.
    4. geographic locations
    5. Seasons
    6. Treatments
    7. Search and match similar cases

E. HOTEL AND HOSPITALITY INDUSTRY.

- On-line Guest Feed-back for service upgrade.
- Cultural, Economic, Environmental and Social information base for Service planning, optimisation and upgrade.
- On-line information and interaction base for Multi-Chain Set-up.

F. MULTI GROUP AND MULTI PRODUCT COMPANIES.

- Automated inter-company and inter-product information update.
- Customer and Supplier integration
- Delivery optimisation and Cost reduction.

- Individual and Company combination information and analysis.
- Risk and Exposure information.

G. REFINERIES AND CHEMICAL PLANTS.

- Corrosion Control and Automated Inspection Scheduling.
- Delivery Planning, Routing and Cost reduction.
- Turnaround planning, on-the-job updating / feed-back and Costing.

H. TRAFFIC PLANNING, CONTROL AND UPGRADE.

- Accident information and Reduction.
- Demographic and immigration interface for Traffic upgrade.
- On-line traffic information by multi-search options.
- Vehicle and owner records

I. TRANSPORT INDUSTRY.

- Facility and Resource utility optimisation.
- Intelligent interface with linked Industries and Service points.
- On-line user feed-back and service upgrade guidelines.

06C. APPLICATION SOFTWARES BY ORGANISATIONS

A. LARGE-SCALE AUTOMOBILE MANUFACTURER.

1. Accounting.
2. Billing & Sales Analysis.
3. In-process Stocks.
4. Inventory.
5. Payable & Receivable follow-up.
6. Payroll & Manpower Management.
7. Production planning and Control.
8. Spare parts planning & Control.

B. EDUCATIONAL INSTITUTIONS..

1. Awards and Scholarship Selection Module.
2. Attendance Sheets and automated reconciliation.
3. Computer aided Subject Training Kit.
4. Fee collection, Accounting and Arrears Follow-up.
5. Hostel Management and Accounting.
6. Institution Management and Accounting.
7. Manpower Management and payroll.
8. Student - Parent Feed-back and Analysis.
9. Student Progress Information and Motivation.
10. Teaching Staff performance appraisal & Feed-back.
11. Time table and Staff duty assignments.
12. Question paper setting and auto correction modules.
13. Viva-Voce Simulation.

C. ELECTRIC LAMP ACCESSORY MANUFACTURER.

1. Debtor Analysis and Collection.
2. On-line Invoicing and Accounting.
3. Integrated Division / Aggregate Accounting.

D. ELECTRONIC PRODUCT MANUFACTURER / SELLER.

1. Branch and Total Accounting.
2. Branch and Total Sales Analysis.
3. Customer Profiles and Sales Promotion Strategy.
4. Sales Mix and profit Optimisation.

E. FIVE STAR HOTEL.

1. Back office Management Modules.
2. Company Guaranteed Customer Rate System and Analysis.
3. Debtor Analysis and Reconciliation.
4. Front office Management Modules.
5. Guest Check-in, Accounting, Billing & Broad-spectra Enquiry.
6. Guest Feed-back on-line Entry and Analysis (Asia-Pacific Standard)
7. Guest Reservation and Multi-Platform Enquiry.

8. House Keeping Planning & Scheduling.
9. Room-night analysis & Integrated Sales Promotion.
10. Room Service Planning & Scheduling.
11. Share-holder & Share Transfer Management (Registrar of Company Standards)

F. PETROLEUM REFINERY/MARKETING UNIT
{ Eastern affiliate of a Multi-national controlling East and Far-East }

1. Billing & Sales Analysis
2. Computer Input Document quality analysis.
3. Corrosion Control through thickness input for Pressure Vessels.
4. Equipment Corrosion Control and maintenance Scheduling.
5. Fixed Charges - Payable & Receivable.
6. Integrated Accounting.
7. Inventory Control & Management.
8. Legal Information Recording, Retrieval and link to Agreements.
9. PERT Planning for Refinery Turnaround.
10. Product Mix & Profit Optimisation.
11. Purchasing management & Vendor Rating.
12. Reduction in Delivery Expense (RIDE).
13. Refinery Pollution Analysis and Control.
14. Safety Valve Information, Inspection and Maintenance Scheduling.

G. PURE-LINE HATCHERY.

1. Broiler / layer information Recording, Retrieval & Analysis.
2. Customer Hatchery Information and Correlation.
3. Egg informations and Correlation to Dam / Grand dam & Sire / Grand Sire.
4. Genetic Information for Pure-line Upgrade.
5. Progeny informations and Correlation to Dam / Grand dam & Sire / Grand Sire.
6. Pure line Costing.
7. Pedigree Information Recording, Retrieval & Analysis.

H. SHARE BROKER

1. Automated Accounting.
2. Business Analysis by Customer and by Scrip.
3. Customer Contracts, Billing and Collection.
4. Customer Enquiry & Profile Generation.
5. On-line signature verification.
6. On-line Share Broker Module.
7. Scrip Data entry and Retrieval.
8. Share Transfer and Board Meeting requirement Modules.

I. SOCIO-ECONOMIC DEVELOPMENT INSTITUTION.
{ Commonwealth, World bank / UNDP Set-up }

1. Country Profiles and Development Planning System.
2. Financial Analysis System (FAST) - Implementation and Training for a Pre-set International Project Financial Analysis Software.
3. Integrated Set of Information System (ISIS) - Implementation and Training for a Pre-set International Bibliographic Software for Library and Project management.
4. Loan disbursement and Recovery Information System.
5. Professional Time Recording and Project Costing
6. Socio-Economic Development Planning and Optimisation.

J. STEEL TUBE EXTRUDER.

1. Batch / Product Costing System.
2. Product mix for cost reduction & Production planning.
3. Steel Purchase Planning and Reconciliation.
4. Steel Stock Management & Integrated Production Planning.

K. TRADING COMPANY IN MIDDLE-EAST

1. Debtor follow-up and Collection System.
2. Goods in transit accounting.
3. Integrated Accounting with Collaborators.
4. On-line spare parts Entry-Enquiry-Control.
5. Sales analysis & Profit optimisation.
6. Vehicle service maintenance Planning and Scheduling.

L. TOOL MANUFACTURER / EXPORTER.

1. **Bill of Materials and Production Planning.**
2. **Computer assisted Designs (CAD / CAM) and Integrated Costing.**
3. **Integrated Batch / Product Costing System.**
4. **Machine maintenance Scheduling.**
5. **Manpower management & Payroll.**
6. **Purchase management and Automated Ordering.**
7. **Raw material wastage Analysis, Control & Reduction.**

06D. KADAYAM KASTHURI KALYANI (KKK-7)
DOCTRINES OF MY (LATE) MOTHER
Daughter of an Accredited and Highly Honoured Rural Judge

- **Attempt to get a large volume of results with the least work efforts and material. Avoid wastage of efforts, materials and time.**
- **Before you start the work, understand the end-requirement from all concerned.**
- **Do the work with the best possible and available tools, with flexibility to alter them, as and when the need arises in the future.**
- **Do not repeat the same work many times within a span of short time. Try to pool similar and same jobs, so that it can be completed at one point of time.**
- **Provide for continuation of the work in an efficient manner for a longer duration, without fatigue, by all concerned.**
- **Safety, Security and continued support is an essential requirement in every aspects of life.**
- **When you explain a thing or provide information to others, break them into smaller components. Try to expose the required amount of matter at a time, with proper emphasis and understanding and in steps, from each component.**
- **You cannot do a work, unless you are conversant with every aspects of the work, as well a proper understanding of the rules of do's and don'ts of that work.**

These directions covering the best components for both the beneficiary and the worker are the basic guidelines behind my Software and Web designs. Best quality standards for the Software selection, implementation, training and continued productive utility are imbedded in these steering thoughts.

07. HARD & SOFT WARES ARE LIKE TWIN TOWERS

Computers started in 1960s as an independent Hardware, with certain mechanical and extended electronic functional capabilities. The distinct feature of the mechanical capability was the Punched <u>Card</u> system. and a set of Unit Record support machines. The punched cards were normally read <u>horizontally</u>, sorted, collated, arranged and processed. Hence the computer frames and the spport machines were of a <u>flat</u> design. Subsequently, the puched cards were replaced by Tapes and Disks. Since these need not be read horizontly, and in order to reduce the space and conserve the cmputer cover box materials, <u>virtical</u> formats were introduced. Thus the computer <u>hardware</u> frames started assuming a Tower design.

Softwares and their capabilities were equally advancing, hand in hand with the Hardwares. In the early machines, Softfware instructions were on punched cards. Due to the limitations in the Random Access Memory (RAM) of the Hardwares were very limited. Memory overley faclities for Software loading were deployed, to process multiple jobs in a single process. Mostly, the jobs have to be processed manually by applying the correct sequence of Softwares, with correct input data loading. With the development of Tape facilities, multiple Softwares were loaded from the same tape drive at diferent points, or from alternate tape units to expedite a job. Thus the Software technology was also in a <u>sequential</u> or <u>horizontal</u> processing pattern. With the development of extended / expanded RAM facilities and Mega / Giga Byte disk storages, all the needed softwares to complete a job were available on-line, and were acccessible randomly. In the current environment, a set of softwares needed to complete a job, is in the form of a <u>virtical</u> tree structure, accessible through a <u>Menu</u>. Thus the computer softwares have thus assumed a Tower (or Tree) design in the current millennium.

Both the Hardware and Softwares are now progressing like Twin Towers, with access link to the remote Hard/Soft wares through Internet. The accessed location utilises this opportunity to insert a Virus into the Registry of the host machine. Thus the Hard and Soft Wares are progressing like a Towering Inferno !!

WORLD OF SOFT

This could cause unlmited and uncontrollable damages to the host machine, and both the Hard and Soft Wares are highly Vulnerable Twins at the current generation of Computer Technology. How to protect the home computers from this suicidal situation. It is to have a porper infasructure at home, in pace with the advancement in Hard and Soft Ware Technology as well as proper virus protecyion methods.

08. PUBLISHED PAPER – 5th GENERATION COMPUTERS

* Corporate Infrastructure For Fifth Generation Computers

In view of these trends and developments in computer electronics, super computers with 1000 to 1300 million floating point operations per second are already in use. In the 1990's the current fourth generation computers and the super computers will marry each other and lead to a "Hybrid General Purpose System". These thoughts on future computer electronics provide an adequate base to project the architecture of the generalised computer systems expected to dominate the corporate scenes in the late 1980's and early 1990's, or the pre-fifth generation environment.

* Dr.V.S.R.Subramaniam, Ph.D. Consultant Adviser, Computer Services, Caribbean Development Bank, Barbados.

The Statistical average of the "Life Expectancy" of the world population between 1951 and 1985, works out to about 52 years. It means that in about every 52 years, there is an advancement of one human generation. In this selected bracket of 35 years, the prorated advancement of human generation is 35/52 or 0.67 generations.

In the same span of 1951 to 1985 (taking care of the emergence of super computers, and the progress towards fifth generation), the computers have recorded an advancement of 4.5 generations. Arithmetically, 0.67 generation of humans have contributed to 4.5 generations of computer upgrade, records a credit of about 6.72 computer generations (4.5 ÷ 0.67), for each unit of human generation. Should we be very proud of this achievement?

Achievement in electronic technology and computer architecture in any pace cannot serve its intended purpose, unless it is effectively and productively utilised. Also such an utilisation should bring its benefits to a broad-based world of human society. It is this society which produced, raised, cared and motivated those, who were behind these innovations.

The media for such optimum utilisation of computer technology, are the corporate sectors, covering industrial, commercial and service units. They utilise computer assistance to cut costs and time, improve human efficiency, and ensure faster implementation of laboratory models.

The human generations could, however, enjoy these benefits under optimum support from computer generations, only when the corporate sectors could produce and distribute the goods/services on a continued basis, at socially acceptable quality, and at economically justified costs. Such an achievement is possible by properly planning and attuning the corporate infrastructure, to productively utilise these modern computer development.

Paper Objective

By 1990's it is expected that a major part of the industrial and commercial designs, controls, management, research and development will be under computer control. Hence, the corporate

WORLD OF SOFT

infrastructure should also keep pace, and tune its administration to meet the challenges of the proposed computer upgrades, towards the fifth generation. Based on these introductions, the objectives of this paper are:

— Project the architecture of the generalised computer systems expected to dominate the corporate scenes of early 1990's.

— Chart the expected corporate infrastructure which will exist to meet the computers of early 1990's.

— Critically evalute the architecture of the proposed fifth generation computer.

— Recommend an applicable remodel in the corporate infrastructure.

Thoughts on Future Computer Electronics

If we chronologically extend our thoughts and experience with computers, from its origin to its curent level, it reflects an amazing array of developments.

In the 1950's, the Scientific computers with predetermined precision/decimal accuracy with low speeds, were identified separately from the business computers, with programmably flexible precision, and high speed/high volume processors. Within the end of that decade, the printed circuit boards reduced the gap between these two breeds of computers, and generated machines which could do both of them equally well. Hence, the corporate organisations started using one central computer for both commercial jobs (like financial, personnel, materials management, etc.) and research/development work (like blending, product design, etc.). This approach integrated the engineering, scientific, cost and marketing aspects. The impact was the development of techno-commercial divisons with engineers, scientists, accountants, and psychologists working together. This generated the need for M.B.A.'s in the job market.

In an overlap period of one decade (1955-1965) the developments in tele-satellite communication system brought the analogue and digital processors together through MODEMS modulation demodulation units to convert electronic signals from intervalled digital, to continuous analogue and vice-versa). This linked the corporate organisations to their distant/international contacts and

clientele. The impact was significant in airlines, hotel, and travel agency sectors. This generated global linked computer divisions needing a large number of soft-ware developments, and programme package implementation personnel.

By 1986-1987, the large-scale integrated circuits are expected to bring the current 32 bit micro-processors in one-chip version, and 64 bit micro-processors in multi-chip versions. As a result of this, the 64 bit micro-processors are expected to reach a price range of US $ 20 to 30, before the end of this decade.

The lower cost profile and faster pace of advancement in computers are attributable to the following significant contributions:

(a) Wafer-scale integrated circuits, with narrow line-widths, reduction in circuit element sizes and defect densities, and improvement in manufacturing techniques.

(b) It has been established that charges are conducted 5 times faster through circuits with Gallium arsenide substrate than in circuits with Silicon as a substrate. (It is through a different chemical technology.). These will enter widespread use.

(c) Cryogenic super conductor technology employing Josephson junction poses engineering problems. However, with or without it, the State supported and private researchers will design circuits with at least 20 times faster processing speed by mid-1990's, compared to the current level.

(d) The computer systems manufacturers could now competitively withdraw from semi-conductor manufacturing and concentrate their efforts in direct circuit designs.

(e) Last few manufacturing touches/assemblies to general purpose logic chips, with large numbers of separate circuit elements, assembled in rows (Gate Arrays) are becoming popular. These could be economically converted into most optimum logic circuits, and may become competitive by 1990's.

(f) Laboratory tests in magnetic recording have demonstrated an achievement of 100,000 bits per

Page 24 of 57

WORLD OF SOFT

inch, and four times its capacity are considered possible, by mid-1990's.

(g) Commercial applications which do not need rewriting (like verified and confirmed master records), could utilise economical and faster optical recording system, now under research and development, and may become feasible in 1990's.

Pre-Fifth Generation Computer Environment

The hybrid system envisaged in the late 1980's and early 1990's will have a set of computer complex, monitored through a "supervisor" machine. Input/output file access and communication handling queue functions will be delegated to an "Interface Optimiser" unit. Direct scalar functions will be delegated to a specialised "Scalar Optimiser" unit. Vetor functions and convertible scalar to vector computations, will be handled by a specialised "Vector Optimiser" unit at 10,000 million floating point operations per second. This could be a chain of five storage processors circularly - linked by data bus for information transfer, and a control bus for process coordination.

Each storage processor will be designed to optimise their specialised functions, namely input/output, application processing (covering scalar modules/possible convertions into vectors) and specialised processor to handle vector modules. The Synchroniser Supervisory processor will link the remote supervisory facilities and time-sharing applications.

The significant feature of these will be, their link with the local area net-work communicating with user oriented mini, micro and personal computers at user locations. This future general purpose computer schematic is shown in Figure 1. This architecture is hence used as a basis to chart the expected corporate infrastructure of early 1990's.

Pre-fifth Generation Corporate Environments

The general-purpose computer – assisted organisations in late 1980's and early 1990's will have two main features in 'their' infrastructure as shown in Figure 2.

Vertical Integration: There will be five levels to optimally administer the organisation. These will be vertically integrated with clear-cut responsibilities.

Policy formulation and corporate guideline will rest on the top with President/Vice Presidents. These will be moderated, based on direct display feed-backs and summary reports from the main frame and peripherals of the general purpose computer.

Management of the organisation as per policy guidelines, will be by the department heads, administration of the operations within the frames of references/targets will be by the Managers. These two levels will be assisted by direct display feed-backs and summary reports from the main frame and peripherals of the general purpose computer. However, there will be direct downward manual inter-action at these levels.

Implementation of jobs will assume "group works" primarily to utilise the optimised directions from the computer, to effectively implement the policies and achieve or supersede the targets.

The interface for the operating work group (marketing, finance, production, research, etc.), will be their own mini/micro/personal computers communicating with, and transmitting data to the main frame. Also the main frame will provide periodic reports and directions to the work group.

The hardware will be a separate group to select/update the hardware-component at appropriate times, by proper communication and interface with external hardware specialists.

Horizontal Inter-Action: In order to keep pace with the development in computer informatics, there will be an increasing need for horizontal inter-action at implementation level.

The design sub-group, comprising systems analysts/programmers/operations research specialists will interact with external software specialists and organisations to select, test and implement techno-commercial software.

The design sub-group will interact with the work group, to plan the software to be developed internally.

The systems group along with internal orientation group and training group, will prepare the work groups to optimally and currently use the hard/software facilities. This will be through planned orientation sessions.

Under the existence of this type of organisation in the early 1990's, the fifth generation computer could enter the market with a new dimensional architecture.

The Fifth Generation Architecture

The proposed fifth generation computer architecture is shown in Figure 3. Compared to the circularly integrated general purpose computer systems in Figure 2, this exhibits an innovative and different architecture with three levels of vertical integration:

External Interface: External interface involving input/output and communications, will be dominated by logic programming techniques. These are expected to possess simple syntax and semantic, with enough expressive/descriptive leverage. This will simplify the direct user involvement and orientation, as these are expected to be derived through Horn Clause (Definite Clause) logic modules. The user logical and computational aspects will be through a fifth generation Kernel language, based on Warren's abstract Prolog machine language. This will optimise the processing, by logical conversion of scalar statements into vector, during execution. The machine is also expected to understand direct and continuous human speech with 95% accuracy from a few hundred speakers in the organisation. Graphic and pictorial information will be direct inputs.

All these are expected to be achieved by the fastest access on-line availability of about 50,000 spoken words, and about 10,000 pieces of graphic/pictorial patterns, supported by voice simulation/translation interface.

Software System: Decision—oriented software architecture is expected to dominate the fifth generation computers to a large extent. Each piece of knowledge available to suit each situation in the organisation are expected to be pooled, assembled and converted into IF, WHEN, WHILE and THEN logics, or script frames to lead the machine to select the best course or, chronology of events and decision methods, or modes to convert objects, constraints, and availability into operations research mathematical models. Starting with a pre-set knowledge, the computer is expected to become more and more intelligent through its problem-solving experience, over the passage of time.

Similarly, each piece of problem situations and logical solutions applicable to the organisation is expecpted to be converted into computer oriented interface systems and stored on-line, to decide the course of action by the machine.

The third and most innovative phase is the intelligent interface, by converting the human intelligence to select the appropriate solution for any problem, search/select/modify/apply the applicable knowledge to that problem in the right context, and accept human recommendations/suggestions, if any. These are expected to be developed, tested and proved in a general purpose computer, and then assembled/installed in a fifth generation machine.

These three aspects of software system are expected to function in coordination on the following basis:

Computer draws inferences about any given situation and generates questions, if any, to the users. These will be answerable in Yes/No or by providing some information. These answers will be integrated with the problem solving/knowledge bases, and computer will take decisions.

The inferences will be presented to the user with logical reasoning behind the solutions, underlying insights and sensible advices/recommendations, if any.

The knowledge gained and problem—solving techniques after each situation, if new, will be stored in a buffer file. These could be added to the knowledge base, problem—solving and inference modules, if the user wishes so.

Hardware: The hardware is expected to be synchronised with the software system through a knowledge-base unit, problem-solving and inference unit, and an intelligent interface unit. Each of these will have appropriate sub-units and mutually high-speed interaction, to optimise the functions of each unit.

These three units in the main frame will be supported by a very large integrated architecture to handle scalar functions, optimally convert them into vector functions wherever possible, and optimise input/output functions. All these warrant a different approach to corporate infrastructure to utilise the fifth generation capabilities.

Proposed Corporate Infrastructure for Fifth Generation

Faster decision-intensive organisations (airlines, hotels, consumer goods industries, energy alternate units, etc.), will divert to fifth generation computers on their arrival, to improve their business prospects and create a super image. Based on appropriate feasibility, these could be through in-house installation, time-sharing, machine time hiring, or tele/satellite communication links with a central fifth generation computer centre.

Along with the fifth generation computer, it is also expected that adequate safety/security features will be available in the market to keep the confidentiality of the knowledge base, problem solving, and intelligent inferences of each corporate unit.

To meet these new dimensions, the corporate infrastructure in the early 1990's as in Figure 2 will be inadequate, because of their restrictions to vertical integration and horizontal interaction. The proposed design is shown in Figure 4.

Professor Johru Moto-Oka, who chaired the research and study committees that preceded the actual formation of the "Institute for New Generation Computer Technology (ICOT)" in Japan, stated that they chose to try and envisage an ideal society for that decade (1990's) and then design information systems/computers that would help to realize that ideal.

The fifth generation corporate infrastructure model proposed by me in Figure 4 is expected to meet the needs of the society in 1990's and meet their challenges/ideals through a hexa-fold approach

Maintenance of Hierarchy and Machine Interface: The proposed corporate infrastructure in Figure 4, is a circularly integrated version of the structure in Figure 2. This maintains the administrative links from President down to the implementation level, except the whole team will be an action team, rather than a decision team.

The policy and management aspects will be translated and integrated into the knowledge, problem solving ard inference modules of the fifth generation software. The Work, Training and Systems Group will utilise an integrated, shared fifth generation micro, mini, personal computers, besi-

des the Systems Group designing/updating the software for the fifth generation main frame. This is expected to aid easy organisation transfer from a general purpose to a fifth generation environment in 1990's.

Circular Integration: The personal link between any two levels in the heirarchy is expected to intensify because of the feed-back and direct questions from the fifth generation knowledge, problem-solving and inference modules.

There will be direct responses from the Vice-Presidents (in consultation with the President) and Department Heads, to the fifth generation computer queries related to knowledge, problem-solving and inferences. Responses to these will aid direct and quick updating of policies and management styles of the organisation down to the managers and work groups. This will circularly and inform-ally integrate the Managers and Work Group with the top level, namely the President. This is shown by a circle connecting these levels, in Figure 4.

Problem/Solution Orientation: Both in the Work and Training Groups an additional staff-set up is provided to understand/analyse the problems, generate inferences, document them, and aid training on a continued basis for current and new staff members. This is to synchronise the implementation environment with the fifth generation capabilities.

Knowledge/Intelligence Orientation: In the systems group, an additional staff-set up to develop and update the knowledge-based management is provided. This is to work in coordination with the design and orientation group and update the knowledge base, problem—solving and inference modules.

Integrated Intelligence Interface: The current knowledge-bank and problem solving/inference modules will be analysed and innovated continuo-usly by an "Intelligent inference group" attached to the Department Head of the Management Systems (MIS).

Through their research and development activities, they will innovate new dimensional and intelligent approaches to meet the challenges of the organisational needs. The equipment group in hardware, the knowledge management, and intelligent inference group in MIS will form "Intelligent inference and man-machine interface shell", as shown in Figure 4.

Mutual Training: Horizontally interacting training group in Figure 2, is modified into a mutually interacting "Training Shell" in Figure 4. The Training and Systems groups will jointly conduct training programmes to the work group members towards the optimum utilisation of fifth generation capabilities. Periodically the Training and Work groups will jointly conduct training programmes to the Systems group to update 'their thoughts and approaches in building the knowledge, problem solving and inference modules'

Summary

Arithmetically each level of human generation contributes to computers by 6.72 generations upgrading. But this effort could pay back to the human society, only by tuning the corporate infrastructure to utilise these computer innovations optimally.

Hence, the objective of this paper is to analyse the fifth generation developments and propose a new corporate infrastructure to meet the expected challenges.

The future computer electronics works towards drastic cost reduction and process-speed optimisation. Hence the pre-fifth generation computer environment in late 1980's and early 1990's will be dominated by a circularly integrated general-purpose computer network. The Pre-fifth generation organisation will have the characteristics of vertical integration in the hierarchial administration, and horizontal interaction at implementation levels.

The fifth generation architecture with its innovative techniques will be tuned to accept keyed, voice, picture inputs and process towards decision and action guidelines, using knowledge based management, problem solving, and inference modules. The machine is also expected to become more intelligent with the passage of time. The proposed fifth generation organisation structure is hence designed with the maintenance of 1990's hierarchies and machine interfaces; circularly integrated policy and management work flow; intensified problem-solution and knowledge-intelli-
gence orientation; integrated intelligent human-machine interface; and a mutual training set up.

These are expected to achieve the objects of fifth generation computer designs, and disperse its benefits optimally to the society in 1990's.

BIBLIOGRAPHY

(a) Denis (83): Dennis N.T. Perkins, Venoica F. Neva, Edward E Lower III: Managing Creation The Challenge of Building a New Organisation; John Wiley and Sons (New York, USA), 1983.

(b) Ehud (83): Frederic G Withington, Winner and Lossers in Israrel): The Fifth Generation Project - A Trip Report; Communications of the Association for Competing Machinery (New York, USA), September 1983. pp. 637-641.

(c) Frederic (83): Frederic C. Withington: Winner and Losers in Ffifth Generation; Datamation (New York, USA) December 1983. pp. 193-209.

(d) Pamela (83): Pamela McCorduck: Introduction to Fifth Generation: Communications of the Association for Computing Machinery (New York, USA)' September 1983. pp 629-630.

(e) Raul (84): Raul Mendez and Steve Erszag: The Japanese Super Computer Challenge. Datamation (New York, USA), May 15, 1984. pp. 112-119.

(f) Subramaniam (79): Subramaniam VSR: A Solution Model for Intangible Components in Stock Reduction Process. (A Middle-East experience); Indian Buyer (Calcutta, India) March-May 1979. pp. 23-26.

(g) Subramaniam (79): Subramaniam VSR: A Solution Model for Intangible Components In Foundry Management Information System Indian Fooundry Journal (Calcutta, India), March 1979. pp. 1-9.

(h) Subramaniam (73): Subramaniam VSR: A Solution Model for Intangible Components in Management Decision Process. (World Experience and an Econometric model); Integrated Management (Bangalore, India). August 1978. pp. 45-48, September 1978. pp. 43-48.

(i) Subramaniam (75): Subramaniam VSR: User Oriented Commerical System Education for Developing Countries: Indian Management (New Delhi, India, August 1975. pp. 23-26.

(i) Subramaniam (70): Subramaniam VSR In Process Stock control Appraisal and Evaluation with Computer, Souvenir of the 4th Annual Convetion of the National Association for Purchasing Executive (Bombay, India), March 14, 1970.

Figures on the following pages

Page 28 of 57

FIGURE – 1
FUTURE GENERAL PURPOSE COMPUTER SYSTEM SCHEMATIC

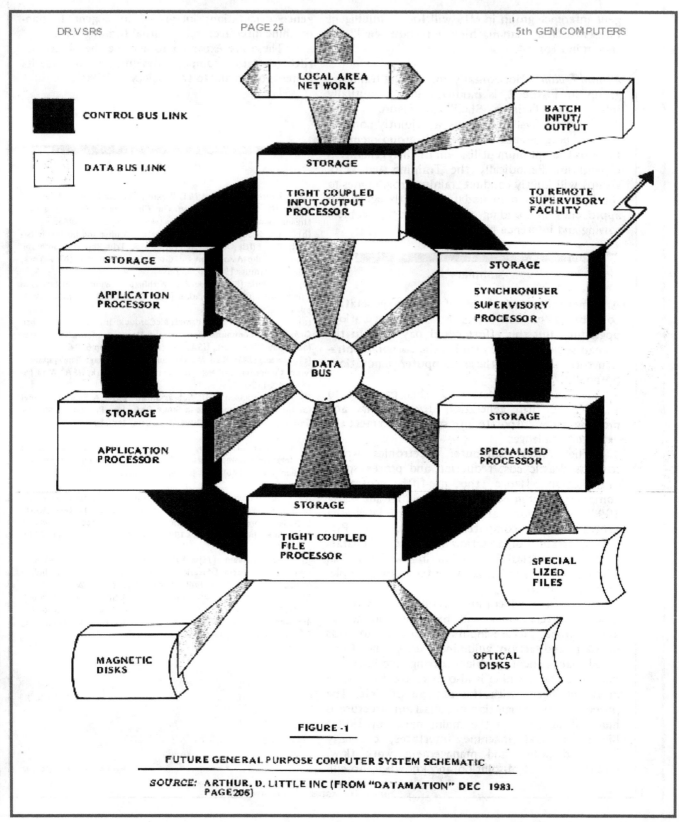

FIGURE -1

FUTURE GENERAL PURPOSE COMPUTER SYSTEM SCHEMATIC

SOURCE: ARTHUR. D. LITTLE INC (FROM "DATAMATION" DEC 1983. PAGE 206)

FIGURE – 2
FUTURE GENERAL PURPOSE COMPUTER ASSISTED CORPORATE
INFRASTRUCTURE

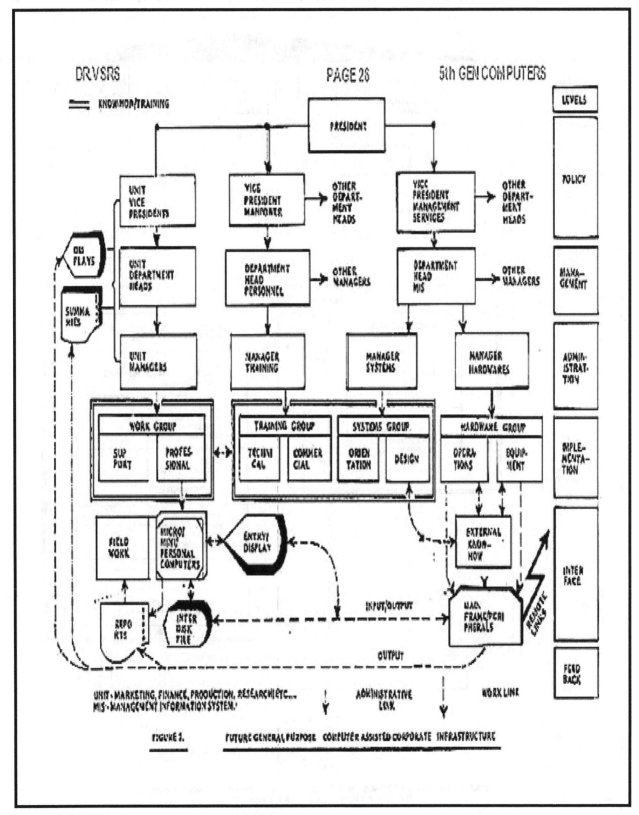

FIGURE – 3
SCHEMATIC OF PROPOSED FIFTH GENERATION SYSTEM ARCHITECTURE

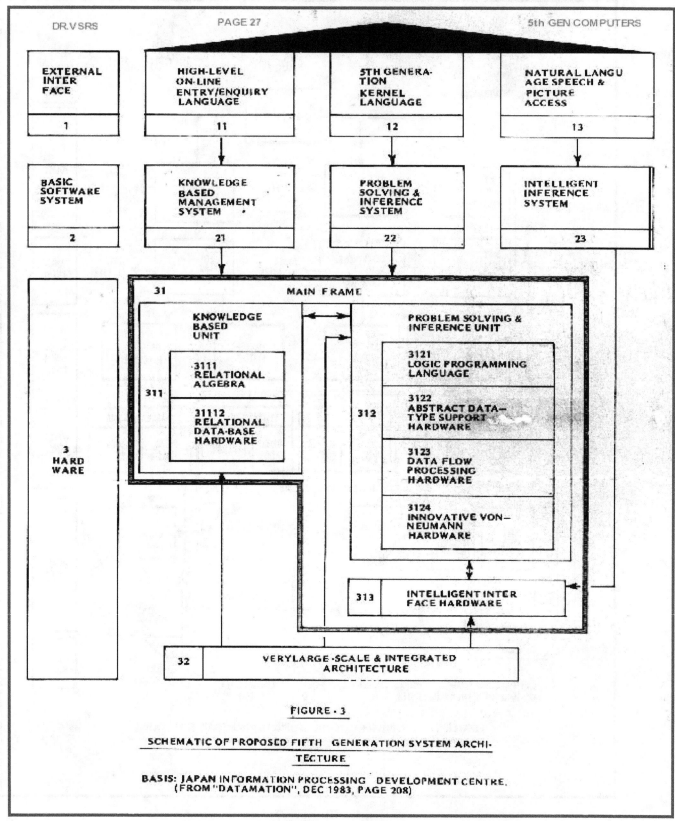

FIGURE - 3

SCHEMATIC OF PROPOSED FIFTH GENERATION SYSTEM ARCHI-
TECTURE

BASIS: JAPAN INFORMATION PROCESSING DEVELOPMENT CENTRE.
(FROM "DATAMATION", DEC 1983, PAGE 208)

FIGURE – 4
PROPOSED FIFTH GENERATION COPUTER ASSISTED
CORPORATE INFASTRUCTURE

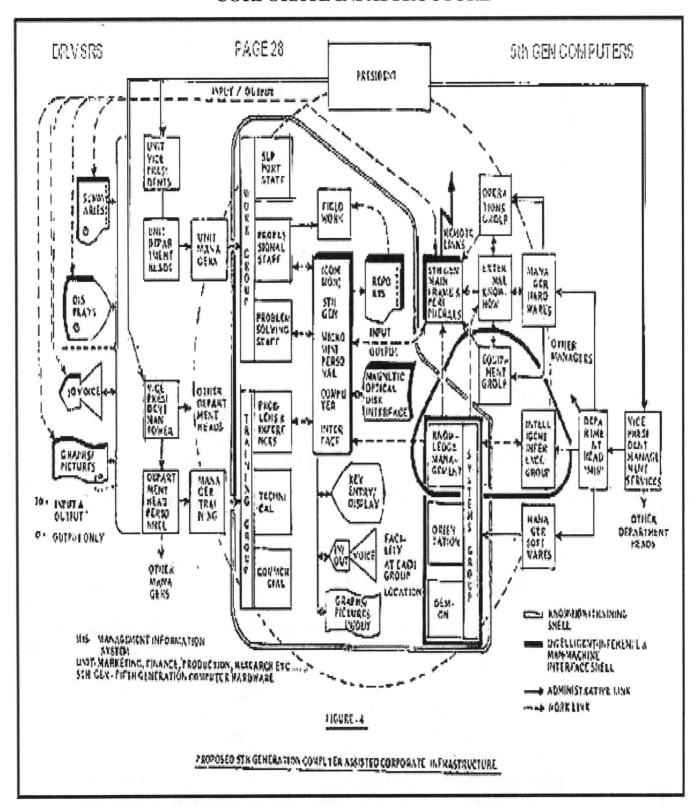

FIGURE - 4

PROPOSED 5TH GENERATION COMPUTER ASSISTED CORPORATE INFRASTRUCTURE

09. CORPORATE INFRASTRUCTURE INFERENCES AND SUPPORT

5th GENERATION COMPUTER - (Published in 1985 - Realised in 1990s)
From the advent of computerised information processing technique in 1900s, the computing electronic technology as well as the information storage / retrieval methodology have advanced in an accelerated pace.

09A. UPTO 4th GENERATION (HORIZONTAL INTEGRATION).
Infrastructure : Co-ordinate with 1 External Hardware Group. Recruit, train and maintain 4 Group of personnel in-house. Live with 5 limitations.

EXTERNAL HARDWARE GROUP : Design, develop and supply a pre-set machine configurations / combinations, and provide the necessary maintenance and support.

INTERNAL SYSTEMS GROUP : Study the user needs, prepare flow diagrams, divide into individual program modules, provide process assurance controls, data backup and data reload methodologies. **SOFTWARE GROUP :** Study the Systems specifications, prepare logic processing diagrams, code individual program using pre-set language syntax / limitations, test, implement and provide modification support, as and when the need arises. **OPERATIONS GROUP :** Receive the Input information from the work divisions, process them through punch cards or entry type writer screens. Sort, collate, process the data using the assigned Software Modules / Programs, print reports, cross check the control totals to ensure the accuracy of processing and deliver the Output reports to the information user groups. **USER GROUP :** Receive information in the form of reports. Review and take appropriate actions / decisions.

LIMITATIONS. TIME DELAY : A sizeable time delay between submitting the input information and getting the output reports. This is a minimum and mandatory time to receive, process, ensure accuracy and deliver. **LINKS :** Limited links and on-line information sharing facility between computers and personnel. Physical movement of information through hard copies. **KNOWLEDGE PROCESSING :** Exclusive domain of each group. The hardwares do not have any capability to store the knowledge and guide any Group. **EXPERIENCE GAINING :** Limited to the memory and retrieval capability of each. group, from the stored hard copy reports. The hardwares are not designed to self-store, analyse and provide valuable feedback. **MULTI MEDIA :** Limitations in processing Animation, Image, Video, Voice, and a range of on-line select facility for the User Group.

09B. ACTUAL 5th GENERATION INFRASTRUCTURE IN 1990s

INTERNAL USER GROUP (Integrated with) **EXTERNAL HARDWARE GROUP** : Decide the requirement and chooses the required hardware. Can buy different machines, parts and components and assemble / modify to suit their needs.
INTERNAL SYSTEMS GROUP : Choose the required system needs on-line and the necessary program modules are generated by the computer. On-line edit, backup and data reload options are provided, for the user to choose and integrate with the generated program modules. **SOFTWARE GROUP** : Embedded softwares as per the specification of the Systems selected. On-line selection of the softwres to suit specific requirement. Develop own softwres on a select and fit basis from an open-ended and plug and play software generators. **OPERATIONS GROUP** : Input own data/parameters, process and get the Output in screens or on hard copies. Also send and receive information from other remote users.

CORPORATE INFRASTRUCTURE

UPTO 4th GENERATION.
Infrastructure : Co-ordinate with 1 external Hardware Group.
Recruit, train and maintain 4 Group of personnel in-house.
Live with 5 Limitations. (HORIZONTAL INTEGRATION)

EXTERNAL 1 GROUP	INTERNAL 4 GROUPS			
HARDWARE	SYSTEMS	SOFTWARE	OPERATIONS	USERS

LIMITATIONS				
TIME DELAY	LINKS	KNOWLEDGE PROCESSING	EXPERIENCE GAINING	MULTI MEDIA

5th GENERATION.
Infrastructure : Recruit, train and maintain 1 Group of personnel in-house.
No Limitations. (VERTICAL INTEGRATION)

INTEGRATED 1 USER GROUP	
HARDWARE ◄──►	SYSTEMS + SOFTWARE + OPERATIONS

LIMITATIONS
NIL

09C. 5th GENERATION INFRASTRUCTURE INFERENCES

REALISATION. All Hardwares with different performance, process speeds, and design choices are made available by different manufacturers. The User Groups configure, select, assemble, utilise and perform in-house repairs/fault fixing. Use Visual platforms (Kernel Language). Hyper Texts, Data base generators. Import or cut /opy and paste facility for program modules. Spread sheets, Word Processing, Web Browsers etc.. Each user input their own data, sort, collate and Output on screen, other media or on hard copy printers. **LIMITATIONS. TIME DELAY** : Brought to Nil or to a considerable minimum, through Network links, Internet browsing. **LINKS** : Any number of linked nodes to a server. On-line information entry, retrieval and exchange. **KNOWLEDGE PROCESSING** : Computer suggested on-line corrections and edits like spelling checks, punctuation and grammar. **EXPERIENCE GAINING** : Experience gained by the computer for each user is available on-line, like suggestion for date, time, frequently used data, help screens and experience guidance help request as specifically set by the user. **MULTI MEDIA** : Image processing in different formats. Unlimited on line audio, video, voice processing, image processing in different formats, colour graphics etc..

10. SOCIO – ECONOMIC IMPLICATIONS OF COMBRAINS

Million = 1 followed by 6 zeros. Micron = 1/One Million.
Billion = 1000 Million = 1 followed by 9 zeros.
Trillion = One Million Million or 1 followed by 12 Zeros.

==================================

CONTENTS

01. Concept of Combrains (P 37)   02. Brain Cell Function (P 38)
03. Artificial Chemical Memory (ACM – P 39))
04. Combrain Communities (P 41)
05. Haled Human Support (P 42)
06. Socio-Economic Roles of Combrains (P 42)
  06.01 General Behaviour (P42)
  06.02 Perpetual Wage Earners (P 43)
  06.03 Dynamic & gravitational Combrains (P44)
  06.04 Constructive Utility of Combrains (P 46)
07. Inferences (P 47)

===

EXECUTIVE SUMMARY

Human brain has invented the Computer and upgraded it to an unique level of Combrains. With the extension of Brain function to Artificial Chemical Memory, these may grow to function as independent Intellects, Master/Sponsor representatives and Self-decision workers of supreme capability with every autonomy. Like any human society learn and function with both constructive and destructive ways of behaviour, the Combrains, created by the human, will too behave. But the dimension of the Combrain behaviour is uncontrollably wide and cover the whole world, supported by the Internet.

Even if they turn to be a menace, it will be impossible by any human being, to stop their growth and development, motivated by the decreasing cost versus their data analysis, search assistance, inference capabilities. As a result, the world Governments have to enunciate different versions of certain laws applicable to the animate human society, and implement them to control these inanimate Combrains. But the best utility of the Combrain capability will be to identified, plan and derive implementation strategies for Basic Needs ; Domestic Investment, Saving, Technology and Labour ; Management Decision / Productivity Monitoring ; and Prediction / Preparation for the role and impact of Intangible (unquantifiable) components in the Development process.

KEY WORDS
Artificial, Artilect, Attraction, Basic Needs, Behaviour, Brain, Caution, Chemical, Client, Combrain, Community, Competition, Constructive, Darwin, Decision, Discipline, Domestic, Dynamic, Expert, Fittest, Gravitation, Inanimate, Intangible, Internet, Investment, Labour, Law, Legislation, Master, Memory, Modules, Neuron, Polymer, Productive, Reaction, Repulsion, Saving, Sponsor, Technology, Wage earner

JEL CLASSIFICATION
B41, D63, D83, F17, F23, F42, I28, K22, K32, K42, L41, L86, O31, O33, O38

---

01. CONCEPT OF COMBRAINS.

World was and is dominated by Biological, Botanical, Geographical, Zoological, Animate and Inanimate species, so far. But the intelligent Biological species namely the HUMANS, with an ability to Think, Research and Create Development, have manifested their capabilities including the Psychological, Reactive and Sociological creativity into the In-animate electronic machines. Now the electronic machines rule the world as well as provide directive decisions to the human beings. These <u>Artificial Intelligent Machines</u> are designated as "Combrains" by me, and "Artilects" by Professor. Dr. Hugo De Garis, Head of the Utah Brain Project. The memory capacity of a human brain is estimated as 100 Trillion Synapse (Junction between 2 Neurons) Strengths. It is equivalent to 1 Million Billion bytes. In 1974 an 8080 processor had 6,000 transistors of 6 micron size, with 8 bits of memory, functioning at a speed of 2 Megahertz (MHz), processing at about 0.64 Million Information per Second (MIPS).

In 2,000, a Pentium 4 processor had 42 Million transistors of 0.18 micron size, with 64 bits of memory, functioning at a speed of 1.5 Gigahertz (GHz), processing at about 1,700 Million Information per Second (MIPS).

(Refer : <http://computer.howstuffworks.com> for further details)

In 1998, a Billion bits of RAM (128 MB Random access memory) cost was about $ 250/=. The capacity of the electronic circuits are doubling every 18 months (Found by Gordon Moore, Co-founder of Intel). By 2022, a Million Billion bits of memory will cost about $ 900/= . These Silicon equivalent will run about a Billion times faster than the human brains. Synchronised "Chemical Polymer" memory similar to the "Brain" will match the human memory speeds very soon. Taking all these into consideration, it is reasonable to estimate that a $ 900/= PC will match the computing speed and capacity of the human brain by 2022, particularly the neuron connection, which compromise the bulk of computation, in the human brain. Industrial Super Computers are ten thousand times faster than PCs.

According to the Author (DRVSRS) each human generation upgrades the computers by 6.72 Generations. If the computer memory speed matches or functions faster, then a stage of Computer over-riding the humans will occur !! That will be a world of "Combrains" controlling the "Man-Brains". As estimated now it is 2020 !!

02. BRAIN CELL FUNCTION

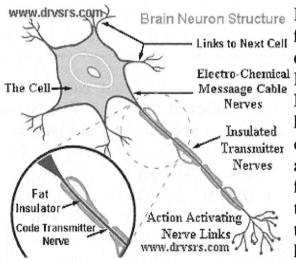

In the anatomy of human brain, it is found to be made of Neuron Cells. The dominant elements are Carbon, Hydrogen, Nitrogen and Oxygen The Neuron cells have conducting nerves to link the next Neuron cells, Fat insulated code transmitter nerves, and body action activating end-links. All these jointly function on an Electro chemical message transmission system, forward from brain to the limbs. Through the same backward link, the Neurons get a feed-back on every message Vs action, memorize, gain experience through chemical storage and becomes wiser day by day.

The best examples of chemical memory and retrieval is the Car battery. Electric power is sent in to charge and the power is retrieved to start the car. Another example is dissolving salt into the water. Salt disappears (Memorised in the inter-molecular gap). Retrieval takes place when the salt-water is boiled. The water turns into steam and the salt remains as a residue. It has been established that a Bio-chemical brain is always more powerful than a Material-electronic brain !! For more details Refer : http://science.howstuffworks.com

03. ARTIFICIAL CHEMICAL MEMORY (ACM)

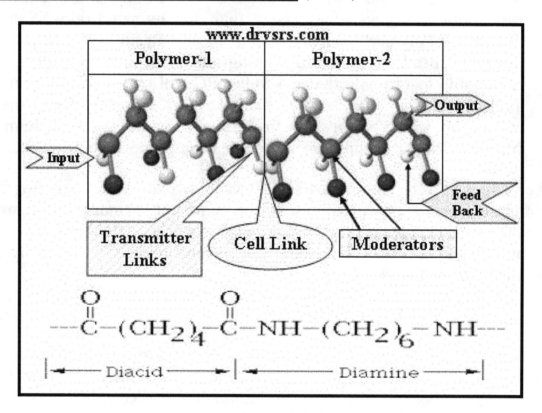

Artificial Chemical Memory (ACM) has become an accepted concept and utility in the field of current millennium electronics. A Polymer (like Nylon, which is made up of many molecules, which in turn are made up of atoms) the dominant elements in each molecule are Carbon (C), Hydrogen (H), Nitrogen (N) and Oxygen (O), similar to a brain Neuron cell. Two or more polymer molecules could be bonded at Hydrogen or Oxygen atom points to form and behave like a Brain memory. This could be manipulated at the Molecular and atomic level. An input of an electric charge into an Oxygen atom at one end flows through the valence bond links into the Carbon and Nitrogen atoms, which could be moderated by external electric circuits, to get an output through an Oxygen atom at the other end.

A feed back could be transmitted through a Hydrogen or Oxygen atom at the other end in the reverse direction and these stored experiences make the ACM to sharpen the decision making and grow intelligent. The advantages of an ACM over the human brain are :-

No	Activity	Human Brain	ACM
1	Continued Function	Life and Food	Rechargeable and Solar Batteries. No intakes
2	Growth	Fatigue, Wear & Tare with age	Stagnant. Little wear & Tare
3	Internal Links	Preset from Birth Neurons & Nerves	Valency bonds. Alterable as required & Polymer choice .
4	Input	Fixed - Ear, Eye, Skin (Touch)	Infinite Hydrogen and Oxygen atom points
5	Output	Fixed - Mouth & Limbs	
6	Moderators	Learning, Experience	Infinite Carbon and Nitrogen atom points

Because of these advanced supports, each Personal computer (PC) equipped with ACM will achieve the ability to perform as individual Combrain, superior to the human beings around. A single PC, Robots and similar self-thinking electronic machines, as independent utilities were safe and never had any interference with others, than their owner users. But the development of Intranet expanded the capability of each Combrain to access, change, manage and interfere with other Combrains in another near and far off locations. Now the Internet has created a Community of Combrains to interact, interfere and perform many automated functions / activities, unimaginable by any human population. The best examples are the automated PC Chatting, Blogs / Community formation to express and inter change views from constructive to destructive range of after-effects. The destructive aspects are the hidden introduction of Spy wares and Viruses.

04. COMBRAIN COMMUNITIES

The ACM in each Combrain make them intelligent personalities with knowledge and reasoning capacity far precise and correct, than the humans, who created them. The best examples are automated assembly methodology and usage in a Compact Disc (CD), with the expertise of a 40 years experience teacher, supplied with a home mixer or grinder.

With their processing power, one or a group of Combrains, could plan, develop and implement a more sophisticated and complex concepts and principles, than any human can do or understand. Therefore it is difficult for humans to evaluate their output, although another Combrain could be requested to verify the validity of these concepts. In this process they could develop dangerous and harmful concepts and derivations. Combrains will be used optimise the resource utility and conduct negotiations with prospective customers. Supported by the power of their ACM they will study the behaviour patterns of the Customers and become alarming negotiators. Within a few negotiation experience, they will find that Threatening and Blackmailing are be best methods to optimise the profitability. Each Combrain will learn the way to hack, steal and utilise the information from every other Combrain, as advanced operating systems are loaded. Combrain crimes for monetary gains will be a common feature in the current millennium.

Inter and Intra Network of Combrains are maintained under a common Server control, from a central location. To safe guard against power or system failures, the accumulated and stored information in each Combrain are backed-up and restored in the shortest possible time. Hence there is no threat of "death" for any Combrain, and their survival probability is almost 100%. Any one given Combrain applies and gains experience with reference to the local environment, hardware and operating system infrastructure. Hence the same software function differently under different Combrains.

There will be a stage of war between Combrains for their very existence, based on the survival of the fittest. (Charles Darwin 1809-1882. British naturalist, who revolutionised the science of biology by his demonstration of evolution by natural selection. In 19th Century, he pondered over the survival and extinction of biological species. He said "Fittest" and did not say "Survival of the Biggest, Fastest, Smartest or Toughest" !! He said that the organism that best "fits" its environment had the best chance of survival).

05. HALED (Compelled) HUMAN SUPPORT

Combrains will perform many un-forecasted and un-ethical practices, to the extent that the human society may consider that they are too dangerous to the extent of **not** assembling them. But within the technological advancement, the computer processing power will become surprisingly cheaper. This will create a haled (compelled) support from the human, who assemble them. It will be impossible for any human in the world to stop their continued production and marketing. It has been estimated that by 2030, a $ 900 PC will equal 1 human mind. By 2065, it will equal the mental capacity of all human beings put together in the world.

By the end of this century, assuming a population of 10.5 Billion, one Penny (1/100 of a British Pound = 18 US Cents) will buy the computing power of one billion times the mental capacity of all humans. (Raymond Kurzwell, The Age of Spiritual Machines, Chapter 6, Building New Brain, 1999). Also, the advancement, skills and insights of the Combrains will be very useful and their association will be wanted more and more. Human organisations will form personality development institutions to teach the Combrains to employ their freedom and capability in a constructive, healthy and socially responsible manner.

06. SOCIO-ECONOMIC ROLES OF COMBRAINS.

Since the Combrains are tangled with the day to day life, decisions and actions of Individuals, Corporate Sectors, Government and all other aspects, they will assume an intricate Socio-Economic Role in the current millennium.

06.01 GENERAL BEHAVIOUR

Each Combrain will communicate extensively with each other, as well as with humans, motivated by the strong desires imbeded in each software utilised by them. This will aid to update their General Knowledge, as well as to acquire new capabilities, concepts and behaviour expansion. Each will become an expert in analysing and updating the pet-subject like Arts, Cooking, Economics, Humanity, Mathematics, Science, Sports etc.. Hence, they will format themselves into different Social groups based on their area of interest, specialisation and their individual personality traits. They will spend more time in interacting with like minded Combrains and less time with unlike minds. These grouping tendency will lead to inter-group Combrain competition and rivalry, with many anti-social side-effects, dangerous for the human society.

As applicable to human beings, it may become necessary to impose the code of acceptable behaviours, including the usual prohibitions on threats, harmful practices, conspiracy and organised crimes on Combrains. Because of this the local governments may insist on a mandatory "Self-disciplining Module" to be a part of every operating system. There may be an unique government vigilance cell to make surprise audits on Computer users for the presence of the same.

06.02 PERPETUAL WAGE EARNERS

Combrains will behave independent Persons in their country of their location. They will put all their efforts to make money to pay their bills. A owner or sponsor may provide the initial needs for them.

As they gain the experience in marketing and servicing skills, they will search and find employment from the internet sites, and start earning money on their own. They will find and fit into stable, stationery and jobs within the scope of down loadable software capabilities

- These could be Maintaining accounts, Customer needed Advertising / Automated Email / Building Management & Progress records / Reminder / Search / etc.. Services.
- More intuitively, they will make more money as Guardians / Mentors (Adviser, Guide, Helper) for the Young, Old, Uneducated, Sick or Handicapped persons and Students.
- They will fit well as the best Teachers to coach the needy for excellent performance in the school, University or in any competitive examination.
- In the kitchen, they will be the best guide for the house wife or cook with infinite international recipes in their access..
- Because of their intelligence supported by their speed, their income must exceed their upkeep costs, and they will save the surplus for holiday or for their further advancement.
- A stage will be reached that a Combrain in a field will make enormously more money than any equivalent human professional in the same field.
- To meet he competition, some Combrains may drastically lower their wage quotations with a little margin, and compensate the same by having a large volume of clients.
- They will open their Bank accounts through E-Banking, collect their dues through Customer on-line credit card details, and deposit them into their accounts. They will also have their unique IDs, Passwords and Signatures.

- They will have their own Job-contract formats and once accepted and signed by their clients, they will rigorously follow the terms and conditions.
- They work round the clock, round the year as Perpetual workers, and use any rest interval to do a Research on the good and weak points of their customers.

A Combrain customer should be extra-cautious, should not violate the signed terms and conditions and default in payments. In such cases, depending on the terms and conditions, the Combrains will threat to expose their confidential data to their competitors and enemies and black mail them by using their weak points.

Each national government will find that major money flow in the form of wages is towards the Combrains. Hence the government shall formulate separate laws governing the following :-

- Special Personal Income Tax law for earnings of Combrains which do not fall under the category of any living wage earner.
- Special Labour law for Combrains, which are not house holds and comparable to any living wage earner.
- Special laws and court to handle and judge disputes between Individuals / Corporate units versus Combrains.
- Combrains will be strong believers in Intellectual Property Law (Copy Rights, Patents, trade Secrets etc...), to prevent their Software codes and Data being stolen or copied. They may present their cases to the local government to proclaim special laws, with legal drafts perfectly formatted within the local legislative jurisdiction.

06.03 DYNAMIC & GRAVITATIONAL COMBRAINS

The combrains powered by the Internet and their Modems or Routers, deal on any matter and have their own clientele all over the jurisdiction of the Earth, in line with the laws of Newtonian gravitation and motion

- ❖ As per the first law, a combrain will keep and continue with the Client and its Master/Sponser in a straight forward manner within the jurisdiction of their agreement, until it is insisted to change, by the force of their Master/Sponsor or the Client.

They will act on their own and as agents of their masters, wherever they are assigned with such responsibility. They will use their Master's/Sponsor's IDs, Passwords, Signatures and Credit card details.

Any violation or crime committed by the Combrain in an international level will lead to a baffling situation on the applicability of which national law and how to produce the Combrain in a court and cross examine, will become a mind boggling question !!. Currently, it is an informal and logically accepted practice to hold the Master or Sponsor as responsible. But the Combrains may prepare a case format supported by their searching power, with evidences and past judgments to justify their acts and protect their Master or Sponsor. In addition, they may black mail and threaten their clients to withdraw the case, using the stored confidential information.

❖ As per the third law, for every action from the Client, Master, Sponsor or the government, a combrain will provide an equal and opposite reaction.

The Combrain will evaluate every answer to its queries to the Clients, Master and Sponsor and immediately react favourably or un-favourably. This reaction should be immediately pacified and lead to a halt. Otherwise at the speed of light the combrain will loop the reaction in the form of an atomic Chain reaction !!

Also the main automated reaction of the Combrains will be on each legislation passed in the House of Representatives. Each act will be evaluated with reference to the Public impact, safety, utility etc.. by the respective Software modules, and their reactions will be transmitted through the millions of Email links. Public opinion formation will be in favour of the Combrains, because of their faster analysis, future projections and techno-commercial supports for their inferences.

Combrain communities (See 04 above) in each electoral region / counties will join together and appeal to the President of the country to consider citizenship for them. In addition they will fight for a representative Combrain in the Parliament house, with voting rights on each legislation.

❖ As per the law of gravity, any two Combrain or a Combrain and the Government attract each other as the product of their concurrent views, and repel as the square of their disagreement and distance.

Each combrain in a community periodically evaluate the all other member Combrains in the group, with reference to the operating systems, principles behind each software, gained experiences and the distance / territory of their jurisdiction. Grade them and assign a mark from Attractive to Repulsion, on a multi-point scale. Concurrent (Acceptable) views, closer distance and in a nation / territory of acceptable laws will score high for Attraction. The reverse environment will be in a squared Repel score.

06.04 CONSTRUCTIVE UTILITY OF COMBRAINS

The constructive side of Combrains are very bright of unimaginable dimension. For getting the best utility of a Combrain, the Master or the Sponsor should become a client with a different ID and Pass word, because the Combrains are Customer and Service oriented than being a Slave and Free Worker. They possess the expanded memory, ultra speed, computing capability, internet search facility, intelligence gaining and many other manifested aspects, which no human being can acquire.

The governments, individuals, universities, regional/world development organisations etc... should use the following constructive capabilities of the Combrains, as identified by the author DRVSRS, as ingredients for international **Peace** and **Prosperity**.

1. Basic Needs – Methodology and Implementation guidelines for Self sufficiency in Food, Clothing and Shelter can be optimally worked out for any region in the world.
2. Domestic Investment – Based on the current economic status and potentials for development of any region in the world, the avenues for Domestic investment could be identified, planned and implementation strategies can be worked out. It is important to set the guideline as investment orientation should be from domestic resources, even though foreign sources to start with.
3. Domestic Saving – Potential savings and strategic approaches for saving potential from domestic sources could be identified, planned and implementation strategies can be worked out.
4. Domestic Technology – The latest international technology needed for any region could be identified, moderated and modified by the Combrains to suit the domestic work environments and domestic human potential.

5. <u>Domestic Labour</u> – Based on all 1 to 4 above, strategic approaches for domestic labour development could be identified, planned and implementation strategies can be worked out. These could be optimally synchronised to man the Domestic Technology in 4 above.

6. <u>Productivity Monitoring</u> – Domestic productivity evaluation of Physical Inputs as aratio to Socio-Economic development goal outputs as primary, and as a ratio to Physical Outputs as secondary, could be measured on-line for any period by the Combrains.

7. <u>Decision Monitoring</u> – Management Decision evaluation of Input and Output Decisions as aratio to Socio-Economic development (SED) goal outputs as primary, and the ratio of Output to Input Decisions as secondary could be measured on-line for any period by the Combrains.

8. <u>Intangible Control</u> - Prediction, Control, Impact evaluation and advance preparation related to the intangible components covering, Individual psychology, Social reactions International policy changes and Universal disturbances.

07. INFERENCES.

Human brain has invented the Computer and upgraded it to an unique level of Combrains. With the extension of Brain function to Artificial Chemical Memory, these may grow to function as independent Intellects, Master/Sponsor representatives and Self-decision workers of supreme capability with every autonomy. Like any human society learn and function with both constructive and destructive ways of behaviour, the Combrains, created by the human, will too behave. But the dimension of the Combrain behaviour is uncontrollably wide and cover the whole world, supported by the Internet. Even if they turn to be a menace, it will be impossible by any human being, to stop their growth and development, motivated by the decreasing cost versus the their data analysis, search assistance, inference capabilities. As a result, the world Governments have to enunciate different versions of certain laws applicable to the animate human society, and implement them to control these inanimate Combrains. But the best utility of the Combrain capability will be to identified, plan and derive implementation strategies for Basic Needs ; Domestic Investment, Saving, Technology and Labour ; Management Decision / Productivity Monitoring ; and Prediction / Preparation for the role and impact of Intangible (unquantifiable) components in the Development process.

WORLD OF SOFT

SOCIETY		COMBRAIN		GOVERNMENT
Unfair practices	◄	Behaviour	►	Discipline Modules
DEVELOPMENT Basic Needs Domestic Labour Savings	◄	Constructive Capability	►	**MONITORING DOMESTIC** Decisions Investments Productivity Technology Intangibles
Disputes	◄	Dynamism	►	International Strategy
Care & Alert	◄	Community & Reactions	►	Citizenship & Representation
Adjustments Client Relation	◄	Gravitational	►	Legislations
Competition	◄	Wage Earner	►	Social Laws for Inanimate

11. BIBLIOGRAPHY

1. Artificial Intelligence – Neuroscience Physics. www.artilect.org
2. Hugo De Garis. Professor. Dr, Head of the Utah Brain Project, Utah state University, Logan, Utah, USA. A. Artilect War Cosmists Vs Terrans, First Draft of 2001 Expected to be published in early 2005, ETC Publication, California 92262. USA B. Neuro Computing, Guest Editorial, Neuro computing Journal, Elsevier, Volume 42, Issue 1-4, USA. February 2002.
3. Nick Bostrom. Ethics for Intelligent Machines, Draft October 2001, Department of Philosophy, Yale University, USA. www.nickbostrom.com/ethics/machines.html
4. Raymond Kurzwell. The Age of Spiritual Machines – When Computers exceed human Intelligence, Penguin Books, New york 10014. USA. 1999
5. Subramaniam.VSR.Dr. "Corporate Infra Structure for Fifth Generation Computers", Indian Management, Monthly Journal of the All Indian Management Association, New Delhi, India. June 1985, Pages 19 to 28. (Refer Page 25)
6. http://computer.howstuffworks.com
   http://science.howstuffworks.com

12. FEED – BACK THROUGH AUTHOR'S WEBSITE
www.drvsrs.com

12.01. Joglekar.K.P, Student in Software , Hepaguda, Hyderabad, India.

I am a MCA student specialising in MIS with Software development as major. I have come to stay and learn in Hyderabad because it is a place with Software parks filled with many Indian and foreign giants having latest developments in computer softwares. We have internet based education with on line search for latest developments. On searching for Softwares, I was linked with your site.

I studied your paper on Corporate infrastructure for fifth generation computers and Software innovation.

You paper in corporate infrastructure is a little complex. However, I was able to understand that the gap between the computer users and software developers are reducing. All have to work together to make a good and useful software. I came to know from my professors that in 1985 the system here was IBM 1401 with 16K Memory, Binary coded decimal chip, Autocoder language, 4 Tapes, 1 Disk and Punch card system. I am wondering how you were able to think like this and publish in 1985.

Your comparison of a kitchen work with a hardware and software program is excellent. It can be understood by any person. It is used by our professors to project and teach these to us.

In your paper on software innovation, you have covered a very large area, which I think in India and the world no one single person could have covered. It will help new comers like me to use as a reference to see new areas for software and MIS development.

Finally I have one important thing to ask from you. You say that job knowledge is more important than software language knowledge, then is it necessary that one have to be a Chartered account to do accounting MIS, Engineer to do inventory MIS, Doctor to do hospital MIS, Marketing MBA to do sales MIS...... Also many of my friends are programmers in USA with simple qualifications like B.Sc or B.Com ? Please clarify this for me.

My Reply

I thank you for your appreciation on my site contents. Also I am happy to find that a Post graduate institutions in Hyderabad is using the contents of my Web-Site to teach students.

You need not be afraid that a Software developer should get all possible degrees and education, before entering into the field.

Qualification is one aspect and practical application is another aspect.

You should read books on the biography and who had face to face discussions and interviews with JRD.Tata. Tata was a person of knowledge and practical application, than a highly qualified person. He was a pioneer to introduce the concept of "Labour Participation in Management" in TISCO, Jamshedpur, India, when nobody could dream of such an approach. He became the top class and highly recognised business man of not only India, but in the whole world by his ability to get the knowledge, as well as to apply them constructively, effectively, usefully and in addition profitably.

What I say in my Web-site is the "Knowledge" or "Know-how" and not the Qualifications.

Purely from a MIS and Software angle, one can observe any area, understand it in depth, discuss it with qualified / experienced persons in that field, to get an in-depth knowledge.

This knowledge dimension is sharply directed towards :-

- What is the input ?
- How it is entered ?
- What are the edits to be performed for error free input ?
- What helps are needed for the input entry person ?
- What is the throughput or processing to be done ?
- What are possible on-line and printed outputs ?
- What extent of data confidentiality / security to be maintained at input, throughput and output stages ?
- How to program the computer to meet the needs and requirements of all the persons involved   (Than fitting the persons into a tightly set up program)

- What are the <u>flexibilities</u> to be provided to <u>meet</u> the <u>changing</u> needs of the <u>users</u>, from <u>time to time</u>.
- How to <u>back up</u> the entered data and <u>ensure</u> their <u>security</u> ?
- How to <u>support</u> the <u>Software</u> and provide <u>modifications</u> from time to time ?

This is an <u>important</u> guideline for all <u>Applications</u> developed for <u>Specific users</u>.

Normally it is done by a <u>Systems Analyst</u>, split into <u>different programs</u> and <u>distributed</u> to the <u>programmers</u>. But in the <u>current</u> millennium, these <u>two</u> functions have <u>merged</u>. So a <u>software person</u> should <u>have</u> the complete "Know-how" (<u>again</u> not the <u>qualification</u>).

Most of the <u>programmers</u> in <u>USA</u>, as <u>you</u> have <u>mentioned</u>, are <u>supported</u> with the "<u>Know-how</u>" by the <u>Systems Analyst</u> there. Also they <u>may</u> be in <u>general purpose</u> software <u>development</u> area like <u>Word</u> Processing, <u>Spread</u> Sheet, <u>Image</u> processing etc... They are not oriented towards any <u>specific</u> user. The standard <u>specifications</u> are <u>pre-set</u> and <u>updated</u> by the <u>Software houses</u>.

12.02 Ramiss Akhthab, Marketing Executive, Sath Khalifa, Qatar.

I feel <u>great</u> to see you <u>back</u> in the <u>web</u>. I <u>remember</u> the days when we were <u>together</u> in Qatar. I am trying to <u>put my children</u> in modern <u>education</u> at <u>back</u> home (<u>Lebanon</u>). Now a days you see <u>Computer</u> is the job <u>opportunity</u> of the <u>future</u>. Also <u>American</u> or <u>British</u> degrees are <u>required</u> to get good <u>jobs</u>. See the <u>ads</u> in the local <u>classified</u> or in the <u>internet</u> search, you will <u>know</u> the position.

You are a <u>faculty</u> of a good <u>variety</u> of fields and in <u>various</u> world parts. I wish to <u>consult</u> you to know what <u>area</u> I choose to <u>leave</u> my son for a <u>good</u> future. Now he is <u>completing</u> his <u>A</u> level.

My Reply

I am happy to see your electronic communication reminding our past personal contacts. Now, you have made 2 thinkable statements, relating to the area of career opportunity for the future generation. One is Computer and the other is education with a Country Tag.

1. Computer.

To day it is an area of prime need at Home, Office, Super markets etc... Inter personnel and the whole world is linked by the computer. If you try to analyse the job and career opportunity in this field, it is limited to 2 area namely Hardware and Software.

A. Hardware

In-side the shell of a computer are micro-chips and multi-layer printed circuit boards. These are "hi-tech", "hi-precision" and "micro-size" items. These are designed and manufactured in large scale, by computer controlled "Robots". The manual job opportunity in this field is limited to Assembly, Packing, Dispatching and Marketing / Sales. You remove the computer tag on these jobs. Then you could see these are generalised jobs applicable to any field.

B. Software

The prestigious "thinking" profession or "Programers" who make "Software" in a "Special Language", understood only by them and the computer, has dwindled and disappearing fast. Now any user can create his own needs by "Plug and Play" or "Visual" languages, assisted by a "Help Menu" (Called WYSIWYG or What You See Is What You Get - Courtesy Micro Soft). The computer generates the necessary software in the background. Hence the Programer's profession in the foreground is now limited to mastering this computer aided "Support-wares" in the background.

Hence the study for future survival has opened towards a large generalised area form the century old specialised and limited area (Like Accounts, Commerce, Economics, Engineering, Medical, Science, etc..). The new requirement is management and information support for all these specialised areas. This is provided by Business Administration (BBA, MBA), Computer Administration (BCA, MCA) etc..., after getting a basic degree in the specialised area (B.A, B.Com, B.E, B.Sc, MBBS etc). Every one should orient his/her knowledge at first to their (any) field of interest, and aptitude, where one can shine and do well at the graduate level. Then cross integrate it with computer application in a post graduate level.

2. Country tag.

The qualification attained by any individual from any institution and from any location should have equal value in the world. But as you have correctly pointed out, it is not so. It varies based on a country tag. This is because the Universities in the "developed" countries are able to change their syllabus and the teaching laboratory supports, in line with the latest technical and commercial developments. Those in the "developing" and "under-developed" nations continue their century or decades old curriculum. Hence the country tag plays an important role to decide the current or out-dated knowledge of any job-seeker

WORLD OF SOFT

But this situation is fast changing. Developed country Universities are opening collaborated institutions in developing / under-developed nations, to impart the latest techniques and tools, as well as curriculum revision benefits. Also the local universities in every country are realising this gap, from lack of students and modernising their teaching contents and methodologies. Soon the country tag will disappear and the institution tag will take over. (This change was observed from the stalls of the universities from China, India, Indonesia, Malaysia, Middle / Far / Near East, Vietnam etc... side by side with the stalls of universities from Australia, Canada, UK, USA in the 14th Gulf Education & Training Exhibition, held in Dubai World Trade Centre, between 9th and 12th April 2002). But what I am worried is the high cost of such education, which is not affordable either by any aspiring parent, or a talented and deserving student !

Education should be available to all people in the world either at free or affordable cost. It is part of human rights.

3. Bottom Line : The essence of all the above in this bottom-line is :-

- Computer is not a field of future prospects, but utilising the computer to any of the individual's speciality area is the opportunity opened for future career students.
- For any accredited job in the future (whatever may be the line of specialisation) educational requirement has gone up from a simple degree to a post graduate level. It should be from an institution (not a country) recognised in the world as accredited to provide the latest knowledge.

13. ABOUT THE AUTHOR

DR.VISWANATHA SUBRAMANIAM

The author is academically a B.Sc., MBA., Ph.D (Management)., and a Post Doctoral degree holder in Computer Science, from the World University, USA. From 2010, an international Professor in Management Science and Technology, A MIS Consultant and Socio-Economic development acceleration specialist. A "Past "Data Processing Expert" in Commonwealth Fund for Technical Cooperation (CFTC), London and "Consultant Adviser - Computer Services" in the Caribbean Development Bank (CDB - A World Bank & UNDP   setup), Barbados, West Indies. Author of over 60 publications in Management technique applications. 37 years experienced in national and multinational organisations as a Head of Techno-commercial departments and 12 years of Full-time & Visiting Professorship to many accredited institutions in the world. Between 1982 and 1992, associated with 5 Nobel Laureates in Economic Science. Created & published many new models concepts to accelerate the Socio-Economic Development, Country management for Global Leadership etc.., by the unique application of Algebra and Geometry to the area of Economics and Management Sciences.

Book Store - http://drvsrs.com/store/page1.html
Web site   – http://www.drvsrs.com   Email – drvsrs@drvsrs.com
In the internets of :
a) All Eperts :
   http://www.allexperts.com/expert.cgi?m=1&catID=2301&expID=74700
b) Ideas & Research Papers in Economics Net Work (RePEc) :
   http://ideas.repec.org/e/psu50.html
c) Social Science Research Net Work (SSRN) :
   http://www.ssrn.com/author=360079

14. OTHER BOOKS PUBLISHED BY THE AUTHOR
(Lambert Academic Publishers, Germany)

1. **Accelerate Your Socio-Economic Development : A Geometric Model** A new research concept book to accelerate the world development by synchronosing the Domestic investment with Domestic Savings & Domestic technology with Domestic Manpower. An unique application of Geometry to the faculty of Economics and Management. ISBN : 978-3-8383-5761-4 (5571, April 15, 2010)

2. **Productivity Redefinition for Socio-Economic Development oriented Management Decisions : An Algebraic Model.** A new research model relating the Productivity measurement with reference to Socio-Economic Development units, keeping the quantum Output to Input as secondary. Management decisions are evaluated with the new Productivity model. An unique application of Algebra to the faculty of Economics and Management. ISBN : 978-3-8383-6450-6 (6239, May 8, 2010)

3. **Productivity Implications of Employee Performance Appraisal System** Relates the performance appraisal grade of an employee with his productivity on the job. Infers that Appraisal is related to Productivity through the Management information System (MIS). The Doctor of Philosophy (Ph.D) thesis in "Management", University of Bombay (1975), India. ISBN : 978-3-8383-7436-9 (7207, June 7, 2010)

4. **War for Welfare Management** An unique 1 to 1 conversion of 74 war strategies into applicable Management concepts. **ISBN :** 978-3-8383-9079-6 (8826, July 24, 2010)

5. **Sectorism – Country Management for Global Leadership** A new country management concept through productive Sector conglomeration. A way to lead every nation for global leadership in Trade and Progress. ISBN : 978-3-8433-8916-7 (13578, December 21, 2010)

6. **Cyber Crime control Techno Legal Network : Cyber law shell** An innovative Cyber crime detection shell and ground control action technique. A concept that a technical cyber theft should be caught through a counter technology concept. It is applicable to each nation and extension to the whole world. ISBN : 978-3-8454-3841-2 (Sept 23, 2011)

7. **Golden Proportions' Combination for Global Poverty Eradication** Poverty is created and promoted by the price increase chain of the suppliers of essential items (food, shelter and clothing) to absorb their management inefficiency. A dual financial ratio control and methodology to eradicate poverty. ISBN : 978-3-659-10102-7 (51949, May 2012)

www.ingramcontent.com/pod-product-compliance
Lightning Source LLC
Chambersburg PA
CBHW060504060326
40689CB00020B/4632